The Sound of Solitude

BY ROD McKUEN

BOOKS

POETRY

AND AUTUMN CAME
STANYAN STREET & OTHER SORROWS
LISTEN TO THE WARM
LONESOME CITIES
IN SOMEONE'S SHADOW
CAUGHT IN THE QUIET
FIELDS OF WONDER
AND TO EACH SEASON
COME TO ME IN SILENCE
MOMENT TO MOMENT
CELEBRATIONS OF THE HEART
BEYOND THE BOARDWALK
THE SEA AROUND ME
COMING CLOSE TO THE EARTH
WE TOUCH THE SKY
THE POWER BRIGHT & SHINING
THE BEAUTIFUL STRANGERS
THE SOUND OF SOLITUDE

COLLECTED POEMS

TWELVE YEARS OF CHRISTMAS
A MAN ALONE
WITH LOVE . . .
THE CAROLS OF CHRISTMAS
SEASONS IN THE SUN
THE ROD McKUEN OMNIBUS

HAND IN HAND
LOVE'S BEEN GOOD TO ME
LOOKING FOR A FRIEND
TOO MANY MIDNIGHTS
WATCH FOR THE WIND
THE WORKS OF ROD McKUEN:
    POETRY VOL. 1

PROSE

FINDING MY FATHER
AN OUTSTRETCHED HAND
A BOOK OF DAYS
A 1984 BOOK OF DAYS

MUSIC COLLECTIONS

NEW CAROLS FOR CHRISTMAS
THE McKUEN/SINATRA SONGBOOK
NEW BALLADS
AT CARNEGIE HALL
28 GREATEST HITS
THROUGH EUROPEAN WINDOWS
THE SONGS OF ROD McKUEN, VOL. 1
THE SONGS OF ROD McKUEN, VOL. 2

MUSIC

Concertos

FOR PIANO & ORCHESTRA
FOR CELLO & ORCHESTRA
FOR GUITAR & ORCHESTRA
#2 FOR PIANO & ORCHESTRA
FOR FOUR HARPSICHORDS
SEASCAPES FOR PIANO

Symphonies, Symphonic Suites, Etc.

SYMPHONY NO. 1
BALLAD OF DISTANCES
THE CITY
4 QUARTETS FOR PIANO & STRINGS
4 TRIOS FOR PIANO & STRINGS
ADAGIO FOR HARP & STRINGS
RIGADOON FOR ORCHESTRA
PASTURES GREEN/PAVEMENTS GREY
PIANO QUARTETS
STRING QUARTETS

Ballets

AMERICANA, R.F.D.
POINT/COUNTERPOINT
ELIZABETHAN DANCES
THE MINOTAUR (MAN TO HIMSELF)

VOLGA SONG
FULL CIRCLE
THE PLAINS OF MY COUNTRY
THE MAN WHO TRACKED THE STARS
BIRCH TREES

Major Film Scores

THE PRIME OF MISS JEAN BRODIE
A BOY NAMED CHARLIE BROWN
JOANNA
THE UNKNOWN WAR
SCANDALOUS JOHN
THE BORROWERS
LISA BRIGHT & DARK
EMILY
TRAVELS WITH CHARLEY

The Sound

Rod McKuen

of Solitude

Drawings by the Author

CHEVAL BOOKS • HARPER & ROW PUBLISHERS, New York
LOS ANGELES   CAMBRIDGE, PHILADELPHIA, SAN FRANCISCO
NEW YORK, SYDNEY   LONDON, MEXICO CITY, SÃO PAULO
JOHANNESBURG, LONDON   SYDNEY

Grateful acknowledgment is made to the publishers for permission to reprint lyrics from the following songs by Rod McKuen. All rights reserved. *Solitude's My Home,* ©copyright 1972 by Editions Chanson; *Many Summers Ago* and *When the Bars Close,* ©copyright 1961 by Dov Music; *About the Time,* ©copyright 1974 by Editions Chanson; *I've Been to Town,* ©copyright 1963 by Almo Music; *Empty Is,* ©copyright 1969 by Editions Chanson; *April People,* ©copyright 1959 Dov Music; *Me and the Cat,* ©copyright 1966 by Stanyan Music; *Sommerset,* ©copyright 1967 by Editions Chanson; *Thank You* and *Love, Let Me Not Hunger,* ©copyright 1965 by Stanyan Music; *Blessings of the Day,* ©copyright 1972 by Editions Chanson; *My Brother Edward,* ©copyright 1982 by Stanyan Music; *So Many Others* and *Times Gone By,* ©copyright 1964 by Almo Music; *If You Go Away,* ©copyright 1958 by Rod McKuen, ©copyright 1966 by E. B. Marks; *Gone with the Cowboys,* ©copyright 1970 by Editions Chanson; *The Last of the Wine,* ©copyright 1968 by Editions Chanson.

FIRST EDITION

Designer: Gloria Adelson
Calligraphy: Sidney Feinberg

Library of Congress Cataloging in Publication Data

McKuen, Rod.
    The sound of solitude.

    "Cheval books."
    Includes index.
    I. Title.
PS3525.A264S6   1983   811'.54   83–47554
ISBN 0-06-015199-4

---

83 84 85 86 87 10 9 8 7 6 5 4 3 2 1

This is a book
for my brother Edward.

We come into the world alone
we go away the same.
We're meant to spend the interval
                    in closeness
but it's a long way
between the morning and the evening.

Contents

UNDER CAPRICORN

AUTHOR'S NOTE

These poems were written from 1980 to 1983, in California and Australia. "Cloud Valley" appeared in *The Beautiful Strangers* in a slightly different form. "The Front-Yard Squirrel" was first published in *Folio, The Quarterly Journal of Poetry*.

The earliest lyric contained in *Eighteen Songs* was written in 1958 and the latest, 1982. Jacques Brel wrote the music and the French lyric to *If You Go Away* (Ne Me Quitte Pas). The music for *Solitude's My Home* (Ma Solitude) and *Blessings of the Day* (Une Blessure) is by Georges Moustaki. Leo Ferré wrote the French lyric and music for *About the Time* (Avec le Temps). Michel Sardou is the composer of the music for *My Brother Edward*. Music for the remaining lyrics was composed by me. Twelve of the lyrics collected here were rerecorded last year in Sydney and released in an album entitled *After Midnight*.

The California House

Notes from the California House

The house keeps changing. A crack zigzags across the
bedroom ceiling deliberately disturbing the symmetry of
this old room, confirming the lack of permanence in
anything.

Change does not confine itself to structures—it extends
to all the outside acreage. In the backyard, high up on
the tallest fern, a hummingbird has built a nest midway
on a swaying frond, out of reach of preying cats, flying
squirrels and birds of greater size. Two eggs have
hatched and two mouths, larger than the chicks, stay
open like a garden gate. The mother hovers stationary in
the air—her jaws a-puff with stolen nectar. Bumblebees
above dive into hollyhock like kamikaze with a steady
aim. Snails leave tracks that brown birds follow. Brown
and yellow butterflies turn every branch or limb they
light on into glamour. They sway on poppy rims and
bathe in open morning glory.

A year ago, I stopped encouraging the neighbors' cats
coming to the house for midnight snacks and hearty
brunch. Coyotes had begun to move down from the
higher hills, their dens and jogging paths now planed
away and covered by houses sprouting up like weeds

and tennis courts that sprawl and crowd and threaten
bush and tree. You saw the refugees, slack-jawed, loping
down the road at twilight. Howls of laughter hill to hill
as youngsters followed rights of passage. Rites of
passage.

At first, when headlights trapped a pair of eyes inside a
bush, the elders in each pack feigned curiosity, so too
the motorist delighting in a brand new open zoo. Only
later, when the odd scream cut the blackness, was jungle
law remembered. House cats came back home when
called at dusk, small dogs stayed inside the yard. One
morning, as the rim of dawn was hiking to the lower
sky, Edward looked up from his desk and saw Old Greta
at the far fence of the garden. He called to her—then
watched in heart-stop horror as she, between coyote
jaws, disappeared and disappeared. No novena and no
silent night were said on her behalf. Her memory is safe
with us without elaboration.

The cat door in the kitchen, locked and blocked and
boarded, now looks odd and out of place. Life is less,
and less defined, without the company of cats. The
downstairs cats are missed and daily mourned, but we

have no desire to contribute to the stewpot of the newest city hobos. We forgo the luxury of feline company in downstairs rooms—our concentration now is on the *children* upstairs.

The Blues, shy Bingo and his mother Magic, chase each other every other hour through Edward's rooms and into mine. Then, flopping in a pile upon the carpet, they seem like one unending panther—not dark enough for true panther pedigree. Black Nikki, Magic's other son, is habit bound. He stretches on the cooling bathroom tile, naps on my desk or underneath my chair, runs sprinterlike head-on to corners chasing his imagination's moths. Then hopping into carryall and staring, he demands a journey if only to another room and back again. At two o'clock, not twenty-of or twenty-past, a hundred dozen catnaps done, he starts to poke about and drop broad hints that dinner would be most appreciated. This counting will continue two more hours until the nightly spread is divvied out in three equal parts into three bowls of equal size.

Dinner done, the trio runs again. Hide-and-go-seek and capture-the-fort push mortals out, this is cat time. In the evening, Nikki stretches out across the bottom of the bed I share with him, his head resting on his private book—a chewed and scratched and barely held together denim-covered three-ring binder that once held *Celebrations of the Heart* or some long ago collection I was working on. Nikki's into poetry. He chews up first and second drafts and tears at pages he finds wanting. Critics, critics everywhere—including but not limited to friends.

This house has shadows too, different ones than those that lurked within the same place weeks ago. Some are long enough to reach the driveway and beyond, some squat like dancers resting on their haunches, anticipating entrance. Some start to fade even as my mind begins describing them. No shadows ever worried me as much as substance of some kind too dense for me to understand. I am familiar with and I accommodate shadows of all shapes and sizes. None new or coming can surprise me.

Edward has unpacked at last. He only speaks of journeys now. Arching in a handstand or suited up to run a relay or thrilling time by killing time, he is the sentry and watchman in my life. Concerned in turn about my laziness and too fast pace, my brother worries as he watches me move further back inside myself. But I am only trying to afford and to effect a balance in our collective lives and our surroundings. My head now does the touring and the travel. I have seen enough world to approximate whatever place I wish to be in. But the learning never stops and here in California, this old house is more a seat of learning than a dwelling place.

The April Age

The Great Adventure

April 19

One day you wake up sure
beyond all wondering
that deadlines are the food of stress.
Other people's stopping places.
Other people's deadlines.
Other people's *no, you can't. Yes, you must.*

If you are of good fortune
or among the favored few
somewhere between the first pay check
           and the head exploding
you come upon sweet solitude
in all its joy and finery.
It's then you understand at once
that here is finally friend and lover
you went seeking years ago.
If not true friend then complement to same.
And no less a lover than the last
your arms go 'round as God administers
           the final count.
Stress by any handle,
tension or tomorrow
is the enemy of reason,
betrayer of each confidence

and harbinger of every trouble
laid at the feet of time.

Who can sing of solitude enough?
Why do we fear the word
                as we do plague?
Perhaps the answer is the question.
Must there always be a why
                and a why not?
Only if within the blood
there is no sense of derring-do.

Stress will always be the chain
that holds us back from solitude,
                the great adventure.

Country Girls

April 20

Stillness loiters in the alley
and sends the sound of solitude
ringing and reringing in the air.
It spreads in interlocking circles
like a pebble dropped into
an unsuspecting pond.

I have looked in lanes
   and empty houses
cycled through the wood and trod the beach
and still I cannot find the country girls.
Those maidens in the mind
whose bold bare legs, round shiny arms
     and egg-blue eyes
still hang in my imagination
   a mile this side of madness.

I eat a peach
and think of what these little women
   hide back behind their aprons.
I smell wood smoke and know
a young girl sets the plates for supper.

Flee from wisdom as you would a fire.
Learning tells us, maidens of the mind
                              will not come forward.
But never leave off wishing.
Insanity is much preferred to nonrecurring dreams.
Dreams live on as hopes' insurance.

Time was I sat beside the Franklin stove
                        on elderberry nights
and conjured girls from Sunday schools gone by.
They always came as bidden,
However far back in the head they'd been.
Acclimations change with thirty-five
                              or forty summers
but actions need not be indelible
to be repeated and redone by rote.
So I sit now, quite still in stillness
sure that if I linger in my longing,
country girls with wide white aprons
will appear to tend the fire
and stave dementia from crouching closer.

Holding On

April 21

I am content to count
the cobblestones and bricks
        of backyard walks.

Like the inchworm in the half step,
I reexamine soil surveyed
                and leaf already tagged.
The arteries' arithmetic
                will not be stopped.

I wait. I await. The heart holds on.
I am being true to life
                as I have known it.

And life is never absolute,
it runs on chicken feet
        between God's wink
and the Devil's asshole.
Somewhere in that distance
love is found or finds us.

What matters is the quality
of solitude we keep
while waiting to be found
            or found out,
thought up or thought about.
Solitude is never sure.
It has no sea mark
without excursion into piety
                and disbelief.
As one end confirms the other
so too the move from silence
to the subway grunt.

The rattle underneath the street
proves the worth of silence.

Starting Up

April 25

The clatter birds are making
is so loud and steady
I am forced to turn on music
                I can write to.

I move into the yard.
A pinecone falls, missing me
as I bend forward
to retrieve another
           that must have fallen
                  in the night.
The house again, and not the tree
              is speaking.
Good morning! I silently Good Morning back.

Edward's Birthday

Last night he brought out army pictures
taken nearly thirty years ago.
He and Pete on weekend pass in Paris,
him and Pete on convoy duty
passing through some unnamed German town.
Pete and him out whoring,
captured in the lean-to, arm on shoulder
                              buddy pose.

Having heard at decade intervals
each story set to snapshot,
I still cannot call up the fervor
                and embellishment
my brother gives each new encounter
with the still-life recollections
fading like the memories of old encounters.
His profile as he turns
another six-pic page
has hardly changed
from what it was
            those years ago
when I came back from Asia
and he went off to Europe.

No public celebrations this year
for our birthday piggybacks
except the kind where two
who faced the elements head on,
                    and together,
refuse reflection and a backward look
except at photo albums
            dredged from dresser drawers.
A picnic for the mind in forward gear.
Maybe Cain and Abel
had a stronger plotline life
with love and hate,
those dual cords all brothers balance on
merging in a single blood red strand,
but I cannot imagine any brother,
lover, father-son duo, triad, combo—
                        why go on,
known or unknown to me
that I envy or I would exchange
            for what I have.
A resting place.

Surely, quiet resting place
sums up every definition
of what love is or should be.

Happy Birthday, little brother,
let me snap a picture
we can lose inside some dusty desk
and come upon ten years from now.

Fifty/Fifty

April 29

Some tell time not by clocks
but by the frequency of hope rejected.
I was always my own clock.
Rejection never bore me witness
or stopped the seasons' passage.

I lived inside the five-and-dime
where wonder heaped on wonder
could be had for half a dollar.
The seasons changed for me
as merchandise was changed
from paddleballs to Christmas balls,
wax jack o'lanterns to lead tinsel.

Mirrors are too close to mirror change.
The young heart welcomes harvest time
                as easily as spring.
Expectations are a trap
                as surely as the flame,
so I stayed open for surprise
and I was never disappointed,
not at nine or twelve
or ten years later.

Without a list of what life owes you
to hold aloft as evidence or lack thereof
what comes to us while growing
is greeted with accommodation
                    if not appreciation.

I gave and I received.
As is the way of such things,
more doors opened than were closed.
As decades die and are reborn
few years come down
                    in a different way.

The joy of small things
and what is left to chance
continues as reward supreme,
though life without reward
                    or prize
is good enough.

I measure days now,
                    not at all
as empty as I sometimes feel.
I know tomorrow is a victory
by being just tomorrow.

The Sense of Solitude

April 30

Cherubim, those angels of the highest order,
hover in the alcoves
of old stone cathedrals.
Widows, black shoes and stockings,
graduating to the midnight hood,
send distance backward in a bounce.

Long silences well-meant
to stretch a conversation,
                    sever it instead
as we go back to rooms and rooms and
                              rooms.
Long corridors of nothingness,
great bushels full of nowhere, armloads of
                    emptiness.

Has reason lost its spokes and hub,
does winter still control the world
as we drive deeper into spring?

Believing fantasy to be
the only highway into life
I arise and go into the street
attempting to erase reality
               whatever its disguise.
Like the nag who knows the curve
               of every track,
I am soon back at the starting gate
or heading for the empty barn.

I set out all my candles
and leave them burning in the wind.
Not content to fire the bridge,
I dynamite the dams
             and drain the rivers.
I waste not time by buying time.
I squander it by always reaching
             far beyond my grasp.
I have insured myself against memory
             and being remembered.
Some of us who know
that we are merely fragments
do not even wish to be the whole
only part of something larger,
satellites to something.

The sense of solitude
is that it makes no sense.
It is not condition or religion
but so of itself to be beyond such things.
It is as clean as seas unsighted.

The hourglass fills up and spills.
Tension drags like drops of silver in the air.
We are but unarmed armies
awaiting battle plan and then command.
Some will surrender long before
the liberating troops arrive—
without the truth as armor, they will wither.
Others may get halfway down the block
before dementia or boredom
                    traps them in an alleyway.
A few of us will stay on till the end
and be rewarded with whatever endings are.

I am not impatient,
only weary of an afternoon
when progress has not taken up
and carried on its shoulder
                    the flag of pride.

Mornings with Bingo

May 5

Bingo blinks
and pats my face.
Breakfast time.
I stay still, barely breathe
aware that my first twitch
          will start the morning.
This game is played out every day.

Nikki, fat and lazy,
sets his brother to it.
I arise, still sleeping
and struggle through a feline maze,
like time, intent on tripping me.
I put the coffee on, go down the hall,
look in on Edward, find him,
already up and hiding
in the second section of the *Times*.
I retrieve what he's already read
and balancing coffee cup and papers
settle on the couch before the fire
          to begin the day.

Bingo helps me with the crossword
and then distracted by a bug
he executes a clean half-gainer to the floor
          to paw his prey.

Valentines

May 15

A scissor wind
is cutting at the backyard eaves.
Larks fly in and out amid confusion
the darling buds of May gone mad.
I meet with my tormentor
and discover him to be myself,
valentines have started coming
out of season and without signatures.
Great bunches of white lilac
bowers of plum buds open as I watch,
grass grows at every sidewalk's end
coming up from concrete cracks.

Philosophers fall forward in a heap
confounded by the honeybees' selectivity
in choosing just which petal to pillage.
The rain is finished. Perhaps for always.
I see Whitman, Poe and Dickinson
trying to cross the same narrow bridge
each refusing to give way to the other.

Hunter's Point

May 17

Street girls wave.
Their propositions interlock
until they form a single sentence.
The bowed head and the steady gait
past the poised and the predictable
           earns me epithets
like wide graffiti on a shithouse wall.
No subtleties like penciled paragraphs
on mortar in between the toilet tile exist.
Streets empty but a week ago
now teem with awkward animals
coming into light from hibernation.

A year contributes amply to the competition.

The Front-Yard Squirrel

May 19

The front-yard squirrel
is stealing oranges.
He crabs and chitchats
             to himself,
then threading through and
into leaves and branches
he spies an orange
three times his head size.
Arching like an acrobat
and tumbling like a tumbler,
his back toes wound around a limb,
he swings out toward
his would-be catch
as graceful as a gymnast in a tournament.

Aha! He grasps his heavy beachball
and steadies in a perfect arch.

Hanging for a moment
with his underside exposed
                to street and sky,
then with a quick decisive snap
he twists the sphere from off the branch.
Dangling like deadfall
with his early morning catch,
he bends back up
with strain but no uncertainty
till finally he's walking on two legs
back through the green to safer limbs.

Thud. His morning feast
                has fallen
and splashed upon the driveway,
it rocks a moment
then lies still.

Such a chattering
pervades the morning air—
a friend begins to chatter back.
The front-yard squirrel
does not engage in conversation.
Back to work.
He settles on a golden globe
          much higher up
and with a new determination
begins his high-wire act again.
An orange for breakfast
before the noon sun signals luncheon.

Day Trip

May 21

The waves roll in eye high.
Every house within the ocean's reach
                    has boarded windows
Whole families, like moles
darted to and from the road last night
to make a hasty sandbag wall.
I see the water from some distance
having come out on the bluffs
                              to walk.
A chilling air
like Sausalito in November
or Zandvoort not wishing to let go
                    of Holland winter.

Seagulls scream at pigeons with a fury.
The rain has darkened everything.
Foreign thunder comes in closer.
                    Let it rain.

Castle Keep

May 22

I awaken in terror.
       What lunacy is this?
Surely not the drunkard's dream.
And yet such frenzy and confusion.
Bombs are going off.
My right eye slides above my left.
A bus runs out of breath
toward a stoplight at the bed's edge,
doesn't make it and falls down—
flat as Cinderella's coach at one A.M.
Pieces of pictures roll over and over
                  on the television
                  screen.
A flea market opens in the fireplace,
becomes a catacomb and then a bathhouse.
Am I supposed to recognize these muscles
                coming through the
                floorboards?

The highway in the bone grows still.

Summer

Summer Games

May 29

They swoop at you like larks
or quarterbacks in forward runs
of either sex or neither sex
without formation or a plan;
unless the worked-out play
is to make the lonesome cry
                        or cry out,
cause the looker-on to weep
at glimpses and snippets
                of great beauty
in long distance runner
or the smile of loping jogger—
here then gone forever in the crowd.
Headband, headset firm in place,
dodging honking autos and the cursing tourist,
hearing music from some other sphere.

Distant eyes and yet aware, aware
of damage done by muscled leg
                and thrusting arm.
Such sleek machinery coming from,
moving from such supple trunks.

I tell you just the sight of them
can cause pedestrian heart to pound,
can set off bells in heads
that were not there or never rang before.

If age-old steeples toppled to the ground
                              at their mere passing
I would not feign surprise.
Should traffic stop and drivers die
                              while shifting gears
As these sprinters sprinted traffic lights
                              and bounded corners,
it would not make the papers
                              or the nightly news.
These runners are the body commonplace
and so uncommon as to melt the sidewalk,
                              wilt the rose.

I would I were the vendor on the street
dispensing water and refreshment
                              to the sweated brow,
if only just to gain another momentary look
at Venus and Adonis too in colored underwear.

The joy to be stone pony on the carousel
awarding rings to every arm-stretched runner.
Oh, I have seen the future
                running in each retina—
it is brown bodies tumbling in summer games,
and afterward more summer games,
                                and afterward . . .

You, runner, coming at me
catch my breath and eat it up.
Wipe your forehead on my chest
with knifelike slash that draws
a cup of blood to prove I have one.
Smother me with arms and legs
                        and piston trunk.
Trample me with feet
that do not touch the ground.
It would be easy death to one
who having trod a dozen blocks on summer days
now returns to unlit rooms
and to such memories that kill a man
with the slowest kind of passion poison.

Slow Dance on the Mating Ground

June 5

You said your name
while we were walking home,
        my mind was on ahead
already settled up atop the covers,
and who you are still circles
in the outside air
unlearned, so unremembered.

We beat down brainwaves
with makeshift conversation,
stay locked in stories started
        not worth endings,
and when a sentence
made of thought arrives and stops
we fail to recognize it for itself.
I would not burn words,
but here beneath your tent of hair
communication voice to ear
        is all but useless
as mouth-to-mouth resuscitation
                        revives us both
and tells us more about each other
than all the family histories
printed on the widest page.

Forgive me
if your name seems unimportant,
        I only just discovered
your appendix scar,
while learning what you are.

Your legs are sentences
not said aloud to me before,
literate enough to challenge wordsmiths.
Your breath tells stories new to me
your mouth puts Gulliver in reach.
Fact and fiction meet
                behind your tongue.
I swallow mouthfuls of it
                while I swallow you.
Whole dictionaries pass between us
                        in a blur
the way the night is passing.

Your hand. One more time.
Spread it back across my face
and feel the stories inside lines
that time has carved here.

I say hello by traversing
your eyelids with my own.
Body conversation
proves your thighs to be
not just the framework of the world
but intellectuals in themselves.

The universe beyond this mattress
holds more danger than a fog.
I will not let you leave
or go beyond my eyes' protection.

No world is larger now
than that land mass above your eyes.

Music Room

June 11

The melody begins.
A single note that spreads
      across a harp like night
then doubles back upon itself
growing as I grow along your leg
and then inside of you full song.
Your mouth now orchestrates my own,
we soar on music from another sphere—
each the other's instrument.
No strings stretched on cherry wood
or calfskin tightened into drums.
           We are only us,
not cellos or the double bass.

I read you with the eagerness
of scholars poring over manuscripts
           unpublished,
written by composers of another time.
We collaborate.
Where your theme ends and mine begins
        is now so blurred
neither knows the source of inspiration.

I come upon three moles
           like quarter notes,
moving from your lower stomach
           to your inner leg.
I track them with my tongue
and I am led to wet marsh land
where jungle vine and cattail grow.

In this dark sweet-smelling wood
let new language have its start.
Let old arithmetic give way
to older kinds of counting,
not new math but abacus.
Let sleep steal me now
so that I'll awaken
in this self-same place,
to hike again through deeper woods.

Nikki

The gulf between the pillows is his turf
until his nightly scratch
         has been completed.
He finds the bottom of the bed at sunrise
and winding tight as any fist
            or baseball
stakes it as his own.

Habits won't be broken easily
not mine or yours or his
and so the patience we reserve
         for one another
must include each eccentricity
he demands or offers.
He moves in semicircles
observing how you act with me
or how we interact without him.
He is curious. He is cautious
         ingesting everything
(you and me in places
only he and I had shared before).

It is not that he has squatter's rights,
he is an equal partner
deserving of respect,
and you will learn as you learn him
how strong his contribution is.

Relays

June 30

Your face, face-down,
now splits my chest in half.
The rest of you is wound around me
                              pythonlike.
A ladder leading out of time
waits back behind your thighs.

I must have rested all my life
                    for this one night.

After-Hours Acrobatics

July 3

I light one candle
with another's flame
and getting up to leak
I look across at you
still curled and sleeping.
Coming back I start to pass
                              a mirror,
I stop. Stand back and see me
naked in the candlelight.

Was I ever beautiful,
          ever young or wise
deserving of your arms or others'?
Head-on is even harsh by candleglow
love handles bulge on either side
of what was once an unfilled frame
that I hung hopes on,
                    never excess flesh.
My frown attacks my own reflection.
                    I turn full body
knowing even funhouse mirrors
are kinder than three-quarter views.

A single movement straightens back
                    and shoulders
and tucks a stomach into place.
Not good. Not good enough.
This copy of reality
is as sorry as the warped original.

I look at you a second time,
hoping I can dive beneath the covers
before you catch my silhouette
                    against the wall.
My pulse thumps loud enough
to blunt the metronome
                    of cicada
calling to cicada.
Safe. I hit third base
            and slide to home.
You only turn and grumble in your sleep.

I do not go back to sleep.

All life is spent erecting barricades
that none of us can get through
                    when love finally comes.

Independence Day

July 4

I am high on how you smell
intoxicated, growing drunker
as we lock eyes and elbows.

The hair behind your ears
                is velvetlike.
My head slips in against your neck
and finds a resting place.

I am dying with my eyes wide open,
seeing Canaan through the jungle
up above your knees.
Let me go now in a hurry
or stay forever half-awake.
Stars and sunspots mingle,
form a clearer Milky Way,
then spill out over everything.

Your breasts
are pushing skyrockets skyward.

Midweek Sunday

July 8

I cover you with sand
and you become Egyptian Queen
       resting through the decades
until a wave comes washing in
to make you mortal.

You hide my shoes
and I go barefoot through the day,
Huck Finn with whiskered chin.

We play with other people's children
helping them erect apartment buildings,
each one with a seaview terrace.

The tide moves further to its other shore,
we sift through shells and bottles, seaweed,
             ocean rubbish.
You find an abalone shell.
I am resigned to one more ashtray
        in the den.

We speak about Australian beaches.
I talk of beach distinctions—
                    Bondi versus Manly.
You say all beaches are the same,
or should be, *sans souci*.
We stretch out for a sunbath in the dunes.
You remove your halter
exposing pale hemispheres to atmosphere.
I rub you down with oil.
Two children run by with a kite
                    and nearly stumble over us.

The Northern Lights

July 10

The cats curl up between us
as we read aloud—
first Eliot, then Pound's Eliot
twenty stanzas at a time,
your turn, then mine.
I raise my eyes to look at you
and stumble in mid-metaphor.

We would move together
but the cats are sleeping
and so we leave the sitting room
to turn the porch light off.
Pausing near the window
to lean against each other
we reach the kitchen
make love on table top
and hardwood floor.
Your ears now smell like lemon
                on my cheek.
We roll and bump against the wall.
I carry you to bed.
I marry you in nightclothes.

I am the pastor officiating
            at the wedding,
your father giving you away,
the happy bridegroom upending
and confusing you,
the stable groom who saw you first
and rides you through the tangled wood.
I smother what you knew before.
No memory will take you from me.

You are my first grade teacher
rewarding me with smiles for lessons learned,
awarding me demerits when I fail the course,
and in a night with too few hours
the final face I see before eternity.

Instructions

Tell me everything. Nothing.
Run the edges off me
                as you run with me
or let me bend you easy
                in the dance.
Delight me with a frown
or frighten me with smiles at others.
Since you are all there is
be anything that pleases you.

Make mischief.
                Make light of us.
The only thing you must not do is worry.

Absolution

Makeup still does not become you.
What gardener would rouge a rose.
Your hair pulled back behind a kerchief
frames a face a postulant might show.
I see you shuffling in fancy dress
        (read black and white for habit)
amid a line of like-garbed women
            into vespers.
Your jigsaw alto finds sure feet
amid the never-ending chant to Mary.

Your shyness even now
is like a nun's must be
when, after final prayers are said,
she must undress before her husband, Christ.
I picture you, the young girl saying beads
        but not by rote,
not mouthing prayers with aid of actor's memory
but muttering with motivation.

Dropping out before the final vow
is not germane to what I know of you.
You must have turned your back
        on convent life
for reasons other than a change of mind.

Discipline could not have been
                    your axle of decision.
Though challenging the cloistered life must be,
perhaps it was not challenging enough.

Knowing where you started from,
I turn my back as you undress
and only slide my jockey shorts down
                    past my knees
after I'm in bed.

August Islands

I light the lanterns on the balcony
before the sun takes leave,
sit outside in sweatpants.
The phonograph is piping
                    long lean lines
                of nearly bare baroque,
crickets count out counterpoint
as though rehearsed and listening
                for cues.

Dinner done
each cat's in competition
              for affection.
Distracted by the day's end
and caught up in the night's beginning.
I ignore their coaxing for a scratch,
a chase, a nuzzle or a belly rub
until they turn to one another
and games too intricate for humans.

Cats end to end
and running relays
as I get up to turn the record over.
The conversation has gone back
to voyages and trips. Australia.
Even open conversation speaks of travel
to the greater island for escape.
Will you fly with me?
Will you go with me?

Warning

You must get out of me
           and I from you.
In these inner canyons,
some have withered, some have died,
their ghosts will push you out
               unless you leave.

Memorandum

August 9

Today I tacked a note
        above my desk:
when love shows its other side
        as it will,
be careful not to term it hate.

What did you give to me
        or take away
that finds me making preparation?

Summer Sequence

You wash your hair
and water flies
in all directions.
I kiss you and get soapy-eyed.
Your laugh is unpredictable
               but there.

Wear the thin red dress
the one your nipples push against
               when you go walking.
Every voyeur ought to have his vision
               reinforced.
And those that we encounter
on our midday walk,
should not be disappointed.

Fragment

August 11

We are back on home ground now.
Smile. Say something. Say my name.
Where is that trust we have?
Night becomes you even as you pout,
          eyelids drooping, Bingo on your lap.
Has any woman, even mothers in the afterglow
                              of birth,
been more beautiful than you are now?

Let's undress each other.
My shirt's already off.

Film at Eleven

August 17

I didn't make
      the morning coffee.
Thus letting still another obligation
         rise undone between us.
You left the bathroom looking like
the end of a long bus ride.
We are at loggers over coffee mugs
      and toothpaste tops.

Defenses move in place.
The big guns only.
Each of us has gone beyond apology
      and final argument.

Hollow

August 27

I am inside a gulf,
no wider than the space
                between your eyes
but wide enough for me to practice
                into near perfection
rules aborning even as you start to pack.

You are trying on belts,
while stuffing suitcases,
discarding one, choosing another.
Hands bring still one more
around that middle of you
I have loved so well,
as if the only urgency at hand
is that your belt and shoes should match
the last time you go through the door.

Insurance

August 29

Horizons hike from hill to hill
and back along the same path
they began to make on yesterdays,
till lines that separated sky
from land and ocean
meet and hollow out a ditch
an army on the march
could pass through undetected.
So it is with habits good or bad.
Certain things we did together
                    I now do alone.
Some things that cannot be done
single file or solo/shadow,
                I approximate
or dream new boundaries for.
In driving you away
I kept enough of you
to safe-insure routine and habit.

Inside Silence

September 21

Silence like a scythe
divides all reveries.
Not Autumn in an eiderdown
or sun spread evenly
across the coldest day
can stop the harvester of dreams.
I make up things that never were
        I acknowledge the abstract,
anything to fill the ditch
once occupied by memory
and the brain's employment.

How slow September moves,
        or doesn't move.
I hide inside routines revisited.

Days Pass Overhead Like Birds

September 23

Days pass overhead like birds
one flock behind another
till every sky is filled with plumage.
White on white, grey on grey,
pink under every underbelly.

One lone swimmer rises from the water.
Ankles flicking seaweed in the shallows
he lies atop the sand awhile
then runs the water's edge
till down the shore he blends into
the background made for runners
to run against and blend into.

A dog is barking after seals.
The moon is up in daylight.
The tide moves further from itself.

One cloud only. Then no cloud.

Under Capricorn

Lion's Loss

September 25

Bingo blinks
and then rolls on his back
                    flat out,
paws stretch up
            to meet the air
as if to push aside
great blocks of firmament.
A lazy dandy lion,
pausing in his prowl,
he senses something gone
(you used to carry him about
            from room to room,
he misses that).

I miss your breasts against me,
the arguments our eyes had after dark.
Every day a new void opens,
the old ones never close.

Portrait

My desk is shedding paper,
like blades of churning harvesters.
It curls up like peeling paint
on walls of some deserted fort.
The telephone, without last rites,
is buried underneath some books,
and still more paper everywhere.
Ring binders and a snapshot of a cat
who could have been
                              young Magic's uncle.
Paper clips, a three-ring punch,
spilled ink and paw prints
                              top off this sundae.

I await the demolition crew,
                    the wrecker's axe.

Sonata

September 28

Summer solstice like a wand
makes magic or dispenses dreams,
in shaping wind and age
it does not choose the easy-out.

Some lost summers rage within
and will not let the Autumn start,
but those found easy to the touch
stay summerbound in memory,
    and more—
they set the standard
  for all summers yet to come.
So it will be with sun days up ahead,
in backyards safe or unfamiliar clime—
each will be held up, measured by
   this one now going, gone.
In a season yet ahead
Some lark will raid the memory
and find that summer
  hidden, not too well,
that has our names bound into it.
A schoolboy's penknife thrust
that leads initials to a limb
and carves out immortality.

Night Watch

September 29

The first hour passes slowly.
I try to memorize the room.
A single bed,
        nightstand with a radio,
a picture of a girl in riding breeches—
all crowded back against
                the middle of one wall.
A closet, bath and water closet form another.
The third escapes intact.
In front of me, a hip high window
        patrols the street below.

I move forward
and raise the shade
        a little more.
The street is nearly empty.
I check my watch. Ten-thirty.
I look again, ten-thirty-one.
Near a streetlamp
two people have begun to talk.

I cannot hear what they speak about
but partway through a conversation
hands are shaken,
        smiles float over faces.
They are meeting for the first time.

They turn and side by side
begin to walk toward the corner.
A checkered chariot arrives.
A moment for the light to change,
                        then gone.

Again the lamppost.
Another stranger, collar turned,
looks blankly at the pavement
or at something on the pavement.
I go back from the window
            to the room
find the radio and turn the dial
until low music mumbles
and scratches at the air.

I sit a nearly breathless moment
                        on the bed's edge
click off the radio and then the light.
A longer moment and the light clicks on
as if by some hand other than my own.
I get up. Go out through the door,
forgetting to put on a jacket.

Down Under

September 30

As often as I've lain beneath
the Southern sun in late Novembers,
I still cannot accept it as a summer month.
Bare bellies at the beach,
brown shoulders in the city square
conspire with pale-cheeked women,
young men in Speedos
                sprinting through the sand,
and Sydney smiles of every kind
to beat me down into believing
that seasons can be changed by winks.
Oh, you summer coming in,
(that I am just now learning)
reach out and help me if you can.
Consider all the summers I befriended.
And now consider, if you will,
                befriending me.

Elizabeth Bay Evening

October 9

I called Belinda. She was out.
I left no message.

David stopped by, later Jill.
We washed down Oysters Town House
with more Oysters Town House.
Room service done, I feigned a yawn.
They left and I was left with sleep,
            company about to come.

Mel rang up,
his voice full up
with Aussie urgency.
Why don't I come out and play?
True. School is out,
but I have homework
crammed in every heart cell,
tests to turn in any minute.

Mel says that he's embarking on
a *year of living dangerously.*
I make no comment.

Other People's Music

October 15

I stay awake by choice
pretending to a pillow,
my arms wrapped 'round it,
that music coming through the walls
is being sent to me.

Then conversation kills the radio.
                The pillow falls
and lullabies give way
to distant laughter
    imagined movement
        forced memory
and semi-perfect sleep.

Until . . .

Forever is not far enough
to throw a smile
　　　　that never was.
None of us know rules,
few stop to question.
If there are lessons to be found,
we never find them.

Tomorrow is the bridge to truth
the pinning and the underpins
　　　　grow weaker every day.

The Outer Reaches of the Heart

November 1

The outer reaches of the heart
are never fully tracked
but I have seen the limits
of my own heart in the distance
and I now know its boundaries
to be unlimited.
I had begun to feel
that sorrows fought and conquered
could not touch or threaten me again,
but this new grief is wider
than the sleep of reason.

I have moved through solitaire
to some new unnamed place
                    beyond alone
and I am stranded here without a map.
I wish that I had not gone
swimming in the distance
without an island or a raft
as harbour or safe floating place.

The afterwish
is always harder to make so
than the dream we call a starting place.
Safety always lies *out there.*

How to get from here to there,
                              the question.
The answer, wait for transportation.

Under Capricorn

November 3

Desperation is the saddle,
not the clean broom sweeping.
It is the yoke so stringent
that no farmer would permit its use.
The rivet gun that shoots out hate.
The chain saw cutting life in two.
Desperation is to death
            what medals are to heroes—
                  condiment, proof.

The Great Divide is not a land mass
            Capricorn drives
            through.
It is the highway
leading from the soul into oblivion.

Spencer's Mountains

November 9

Spencer's laugh could light a fire.
He picks me up half after ten
and we begin to dribble back and forth
through Sydney's fifth world bars.
So many beautiful people, so little time.
So much to pull you in and under
                              if you stumble.

Spence is on the dance floor
slam-dancing with a grey-black girl.
                    They sway like scarecrows,
bird dancers pulling
at their cornstalk bodies.
A drag queen asks me if I boogie.
                              I say *no*, then *yes*,
and we are only one more couple
                    in the carnival.
She takes my shirt off,
without suggestion, I remove my pants.
In sagging shorts, I grind and bump—
                              a reject from burlesque.
The night becomes
a double neon weave.

I spot my disappearing trousers
dissolving in a conga line,
retrieve and pull them up and on.
A deathtrap ride through trumpet traffic,
then in and out of seven pubs
                    within a single block.

Children on the prowl
                    open to the moment.
The moment comes.
She looks like Sunday afternoon,
lazy golden arms, a deeper bronze at
                                    elbows,
hair pulled back and knotted in a triad
then falling loosely at her shoulders.
The top half of her breasts are open to the night
the other half is pushing yellow bibbing
                                    to get free.

She looks at me. I cannot speak.
Forever runs by in a blink.
I am conveyed by spiritkind
through and into unnamed tunnels.

People crowd us
        come between us.
I hold my breath and will her back.
Then as things happen, that fail to happen,
she fades, she falls, she flies.
I try to follow,
duck, dart, stand on tiptoe, stretching up
to see if she is still eyewindow. No.
I hit the door inside a rush,
                she is not on the street.
The moment dies
without the hope of resurrection.

Again I twist amid the maze
like some demonic kite tail
spiraling from heaven to the ground.

Boy George has caught a lyric line
and holds it by its ears
up between the woofer and the tweeter—
he frees it only after strangulation.

Spence eyes two couples.
Spreads my bets, he says.
I watch them fence
like ruffled grouse,
all eyes and eyelids
        down and up,
until the foursome,
given common ground by Spencer,
                leave together.
He shrugs and says, *Let's eat.*
To him that means
skewered wienies dipped in Vegemite,
          disease upon a stick.

The night is on its axis nearing dawn.
Am I on high or in an annex?
Is hell three wishes past
        or three to come?
Sweet Sydney heading unto Sunday
a beat away from morning papers
          thrown to street
and milkman's goods delivered.

Sydney is
what San Francisco says it is.
                     cosmo and the cosmos.
Ten years ago old Sydney Towne
               had Sausalito breath
and seven hills not seventeen.
The population has kerplopped.
Harbour houses stack like building blocks
Boats outnumber boating sheds.
But sails on Saturday are still
Dong Kingman come to life.
And though Australian Crawl
is now the traffic over Harbour Bridge,
it's still wide friendly grins
spiling out of pubs at twilight hour
in wider flood than lager.
And love, oh selfless love
is moored at every dock
tied up at every tying place.

The night (and newer wide-awake) mares
                   infect my reverie.

Street people
in their two A.M. parade.
now melt and meld in Mardi Gras.

A man goes by on stilts.
Another man is handcuffed to his arm,
he has to stretch to match the other's stride.
Jaws and jawbones
suck the stars and starlight
until the blackness fades
          to final black
and I am driven hotel homeward.

I bang the steel grate
and wake the concierge,
wave Spencer off
and ride the elevator up.
My room is like a concrete cage,
but even Gideon unopened
          on the bedside table
cannot erase escape,
a weekend pass, a peace parole.

The Road to Yaramalong

November 17

Along the road to Yaramalong
vendors' lean-tos offer grapes
            and watermelons,
tangerines by sack and not by pound.
We stop before the turnoff to the farm.
Caroline is cross about the weather
            but in love with life,
she bubbles like the new wine will
            in two months time.
She has a way of drawling my first name
            into two syllables.
We buy some onions.

When Cloud Valley rises in the windscreen,
I am unprepared for it.
The jungle seems much closer to the yard,
the deer have multiplied.
The veranda is now overgrown with vine.
All the fields are planted.
A hawk is searching for a higher tree.
As we come 'round the bend
something too big to be a cat
runs forward to protective wood.

The sun has not yet reached the perch
from where it plunges to the twilight.
The ground is hard as August in America.
A neighbour waves.
The dust his passing truck churns up
leaves all of us in limbo.

Coming back to daylight,
like patients waking from an ether haze,
I am confronted by true colors,
engulfed by pastels
prettier than painted posies.
This must be some pride of eagles'
                    nesting place.

The Hawk's Backyard

I sleep all day. Erasing nothing.

Yesterday I crawled beneath the tractor
             and attacked the motor,
fixing it by noon.
Caroline rewarded me with milk and berries.

The half a case of black-red wine
that John dredged up
has pissed away the afternoon
and shot off half the night.

I call home. The cats are fine.
Bingo nearly caught a mouse.
Edward's in the morning of a new love,
             he sounds anxious.
He says *you* came by Saturday.

A long walk in the trees
through eyelets hollowed out of staghorn
until I reached a clearing
spared by fauna and the underbrush.

I start a conversation with the sun,
                        am interrupted
when the same hawk I saw days ago
comes between us—
seeking, I suppose, another tree
or scouting field mice lower down.

Oh God, if I knew sunlight's name
I'd seek him out on hill or road
and ride him till we fell as one
in shadows only night can make.
I am the solitary hawk.
I am the lonesome bird on high.
I am the sun's disciple
            dying in his ray—
and I am nothing when alone,
less than nothing without love.
Where is that safety solitude I practice?

In Praise of Difference

November 21

I watch John's face
          in front of me—
by now I know each line
like memorized Millay or Eliot.
Absent for the first time
since I found it years ago
is that practiced-to-perfection worry
                    coming forward
from the near side of each eye
then moving outward to his ears.
Such calm and lack of distance
cannot be manmade.
          It is woman's work.

I decide that men
cannot do without women—
they are necessary on every level
                    of our lives.
A pity we are only vital
on but few of theirs.

Cloud Valley

November 22

Clouds like crumpled handkerchiefs
expand, retract, and then again expand
              within a crowded sky.
Trees are younger here, roads longer.
Even telephone lines seem more finely tuned.
Their hum is not unlike
bellbirds at the downfield gate.

The deer run free.
They trot in herds,
          all shapes and sizes
lingering and malingering
at the edge of rain forests,
where Spanish moss rides up
             the tree trunks
and leaps from limb to limb.
At night and every morning
there are rainbows
that erase themselves
even as I run to fetch a camera.

Birds of every colour
hang in the air at breakfast feeders,
later slipping through the trees
to fill their feathered bellies
with a dozen unsuspecting dessert bugs.

I sleep well here
and Gabriel has come down
                    for the weekend.
Caroline and John seem happy—
she of the slow melodious voice
and languid afternoon naps,
he astride his tractor turning earth,
fixing fences with the aid of Link
or feeding endless sugar cubes to Casanova.
We meet at mealtime
to laugh at nothing
or offer never-ending toasts
            to one another
with South Australian wine.

This turquoise world
feels more like South America
              than New South Wales.
It is altogether too civilized
              to be civilized.

Gabriel is always smiling
a sly half-European smile.
I think she longs to go back home
              to Florence
and some only hinted at
tanned and sleek Italian lover.
I long for her to stay.
Link, Cloud Valley's clever clown,
addresses all his jokes to her.

This is like some idyll, being idle,
trying hard to pressure John
to do more writing.
Utopia crumbles at the edges
whenever I forget to remember
              to forget.

At night, we all play Willie Nelson records,
and make the overseas operators crazy
trying to track down Roger Miller.
(When all of us are famous
who'll be left to clap?)

Last night and far into the morning
I played for them
the newest version of *Black Eagle*,
filling in the story between the tracks.
All day today,
with Casanova neighing
softing in the pasture,
John whistled *Flying Free*.
I have never felt more bound,
        not by circumstance
but by another summer coming in;
I will not let it carbon one just past.

If time were not a trumpet
always sounding out assembly
                    and formation
I would let the work go whistling
and send out obligations with the garbage,
then sink down into pillows
and find that dozen years of sleep
I've somehow lost,
or go to work for John,
building, tearing down,
then putting fences up again—
marooned in sweet monotony
of motion physical without emotion.
I am marking time or wasting time
or trapped by time or something.

Just now, the only sound I hear
is the pealing of Australian bellbirds.
Someone's at the downfield gate.

Mind Shifts

If I could wrap the rain
            around me
I would not.
Nor would I willingly go beyond
            the reach of clouds.
There is comfort in the drizzle
            of an afternoon
and something sure and constant
in the roar of gutter rivers
when I awaken in the night.

Why is it
thunder's first announcement
            of impending black
can calm me easier than daylight?
It may be that the rain outside
drop by drop and drip by drip
builds up a wall of safety.
I lie about security.
I want the safety of familiar arms
while holding freedom to the light
as blueprint and *the prize.*

There is no freedom without familiars,
no safety without the speed
to drive away from safety.

Moderation is but one more
                    yo-yo snare.
I should have been a seaman
                    or a miner,
learning flag code signals—
                    lamp wick warnings,
ready for each mind shift
and each mine shaft down a life.
Instead I am a yeoman
and of no convincing guard.

By Rote

November 30

The hand has firmer grips
than what it gives to handshakes.
It pulls passion to perspective
on solo nights and so low days.

I lie here aching
            from my belly down.
I close the shutters
so that I might ease my private pain
                in private darkness.

Her face is losing definition.
She shuttles in and out of focus.
Next time I will have to let
                    old boundaries fall
and build new guidelines.

Australian Gold

December 1

The rainbow's rim
    is highly prized
but I have trod it all the same
by coming back again to where
wise Capricorn divides the land
and lets the Southern Cross befriend
traveling man and Sunday soldier.

The yawning eucalyptus
        in the square
the daisy in the outback,
the palm that slices seacliff,
each has its share of dark
             Australian Gold,
and Queensland valleys
make the tuckerbag that holds it.
If I have been escaping,
        I can go back home—
a rich man now with Gold Coast eyes.

Leaving Queensland

December 6

I believe most cities
           and most countries too
                      are loved
for what we feel they could be
not what they are.
It only takes another step
to give a wish the outward look of truth.

The Aussie Outback is the last frontier,
the cowboy left in me still sees
only his own image looking back
from all the faces of young jackaroos.
He still eats the long-drive dust for lunch.
And given back the back and groin
                of twenty summers past
he would be there underneath The Cross
night-riding off to Kimberly
                ready for the roundup—
paycheck spent before payday,
his mind no further up ahead
than one more waterhole.

Cowboys know God better than the preacher,
better even than the preacher's son.
They understand the give and take of prayer,
and prize short grass
as much as spring green valley.
Intrigue is as alien to horse and rider
                              as is total loss.
Loss is something to be gotten over
in preparation for the gain upcoming.

In trying to find room to try,
I come back in the end to cowboy life.
The desperate will claw at anything
that helps dispel the terror.
And where but here
in solitude's most solitary outpost
could I find range enough to ride?
This is the California I knew growing up.
Colorado before condominium.
Montana when the rivers ran.
Nebraska plain sans missile silos.
The new Nevada without neon.

The cowboy wish:
one more day of sunshine
      one less mile of dust
another chance to win the prize
          and keep it.

Home Ground

Magic

December 12

On furry fours she comes to me
tail flicking, twitching in the air,
then mental judgment firm, intact,
she jumps up on my lap and lands
firm, exactly as she planned.
She pushes at my whiskered chin,
                        and I push back.

It's Magic's Welcome Home.
The non-accusing purr
is pure electric.
While I was gone
a new trick has been mastered.
She throws a round red ball
                        high in the air,
catches it and bats it
back and forth to Edward.

Nikki watches
like a grandstand tennis fan,
head stationary, eyes rowing left to right.

Home Ground

The house suspended change
                    while I was gone,
it waited.

The only way to know the lightning
is to touch the thunder on home ground.
I would not miss
a creak or crack arriving,
a single shingle
that the wind gives wings to.

Where else but home
can any man meet danger
                    almost as an equal?

Empty Harbor

Those of us who sleep alone
are like abandoned boats—
we become accustomed
to lack of ownership.
We believe our chosen paths
are only where the sea drift takes us.

I have come back
to where the cedar hills
wear darkness like a stocking cap,
where morning comes the way
                    the fish hawk comes
quickly and on silent wings—
not because I had to or so wished
but because I found myself
moving in this sure direction.

I am here still looking for you.
There are no days
when I do not seek you out,
no hours anymore when you are not
                              paramount
when I am not sure beyond imagining
that I will meet you in the hills
        or on the street.
I never do.
But I still go and come
to places we shared first together.
I always travel alleyways we knew;
these journeys need no compass
            and no chart.
They have been tracked before
and I will go on tracking them
            alone if need be.

The Christmas Cactus

December 17

The Christmas cactus
blooms against the wall—
its crimson vulva opening at night
and staying through the season,
the blossoms heavy
at the end of slender stems
of plants like octopi
sans evil eye and middles.

Pink and crimson
in the bath or after bath
hands dabbing at your arms
you were Christmas every silent night.
Today a woman in the East-end market
looked up from celery and salad greens.
For one slow moment, it was you—
Christmas in a black print dress.
I am hounded by the holidays
that come in bunches now.
Bright poinsettias and red ribbons
tied to cedar branch and pine,
great armfuls of you signal to me
question me at every corner.

Heavy-headed, staring down
avoiding Yuletide smiles
and New Year promises,
I stay as calm as crystal,
but I am still afraid
              of looking up.

La Ronde

Call out to a passing stranger.
      Say *hello, bon soir*.
The no-more stranger
      in return
will give like greeting to another
who will keep it going
until the circle comes
      full circle.

Hoist up a flag of gold and green
      Spring and Autumn intertwined,
and you will find each season
      waving to the others
until all four join hands,
their borders blurring.

Take child and second child
      to your side
so close that walking
      is a single act
and you will find one shadow only.

Take anything that takes you
                    from yourself
and you will have less time
                         to build
self-sympathy in ample store.
More than taking, plant and give—
the harvest will be bountiful.

I leave off writing
              and begin to read.

Crickets

December 19

Somewhere in the attic
or within a hollow wall
a cricket and his kin and lesser kin
are moving in, unpacking bags,
inspecting their new residence.

Nikki's eyes roll upward
when what was meant to be
                              a cheerful chirp
disturbs his noontime nap.
I caught him one day stretching up
to paw a point where two walls meet,
sure that he had found
the nesting place of his new nemesis.
In sly perversity, the cricket family
                    and some friends
began to chant in unison,
from somewhere in another wall.

Interludes are badly named—
even purgatory is a prelude.

Garden Song

December 26

The rain's in recess.
I go into the garden
to check on orchid spikes
or roses planted by my mother,
long enough ago to be long gone
or stopped from blooming,
yet not so far back
       I cannot recall
the circumstance of every bush.

They bloom on . . .
not one has withered,
dried by sun or flattened down
              by frost.
And she still buds each day
blooming at odd hours.
Photographs look out at me
from mantelpiece and dresser drawer,
they tumble from a half-read book.
Inside my brother's eyes
       I catch her waving—
she, too, the hermit.
Even as her hand is raised,
it comes up with timidity.

Only lately has this family business
of hermits in our solitary rooms
            begun to haunt me.
I wish to break the mold
            and enter life again
                arms open, unafraid.

However deep this strain of *self*
                        may run,
it must be stopped.

New Year's Eve

December 31

The old year
turning into darkness,
the new one struggling
to find a path, a piece
                of light
catches me between
the shadows just now fading
and the other, bags packed
                moving in.

Snow today. Heavy.
Not ending till late afternoon.
Seers, dependable as tarot readers,
calibrate the weather
and pronounce a lengthy winter.
But the pines still breathe
the grass still shudders
                even under snow.
If the world is rolling over,
the end is coming slowly.
Some birds along the fence.
Finch, I think
                or winter sparrows.

They trot about the pillage
          what the squirrels left.
They know that God
          is in the neighborhood.

Honeysuckle hibernates.
Beyond the wood the deer still prance
          and prod the ground
newly hollowed by the beaver.
Years may dance and do a turnaround
          but little changes.
Even age and time take on a sameness
          with age and time.
If winter is to be a worry
it will not be so within this house.

We are too hidebound here
to bend to seasons' signals.
Not even pine boughs in the backyard
arch under winter's weight.

Hurry, Spring. Be here soon.
I am eager, evergreen and ready
to step into the ring and go the distance.
I will take on jonquils in their time
                        and mine.
For now the holly berry has to be enough
                    and welcome.

Beginning Again

January 2

The eternal magic of eternal things
sends the dreamer out into the world,
      brings him home again.
One wind makes another.
Recent rain reminds us of a rain ago.
Sunshine is the same each time
seen through different eyes,
      felt on different skin,
it is still a wonder and a prize
as love and loving always is again.

I begin today. In life, in love,
      in everything
the same start I had every yesterday
not concerned with where I am,
      where I have been,
only where I go and to what end.

Does rain provide a resurrection
or plow a final resting place,
does love once done inhibit love,
life once lived stop life
from spouting from a dying limb?
These must be winter questions
since answers only come when winter
                          comes again.

Some songs do not exist without the singer
certain rhymes are trapped and lost
                    on certain pages
but these are only songs and rhymes.
Eternal magic still rampages
on the inside of eternal things.
Fire. The river. Plum and cherry blossom
and the vigilance of all the visions
the dreamer carries back from traveled worlds.

I have been thinking about
                    the absence of love.

How useless April or December is
without another ear to turn to
or another's eyes to see
a certain wonder exactly in the way
                    it came to us.

A little melancholia for the final act
a bit of excess baggage shuffled off
an old coat traded in for new.

Nothing is quite
what we think it is.
Clichés become so for good reason,
the best contain a universal truth.
It is never wrong to want,
but you cannot have everything—
where would you put it?

The Cost

A maple leaf lies
frozen in the ice,
its edges curled upward
as if to say *release me*.
No skater on the pond looks down.
          Not even January sun
keeping pace with each blade runner
pauses in its ride toward the dark.

A light snow falls. Another frost.
A later layer on the pond.
The pristine leaf is lost
or held forever in an ice age coming.
I know that if I walk the bridge
connecting riverbank to riverbank,
a letter will be waiting in the box.
Or turning past the maple tree,
I will see the bench
you sprang from in the summer
to chase the crows from out the garden.
I am in no hurry to encourage memory.

I put off taking even one step forward,
knowing every forward step leads back.
Meetings end in partings.
Sunrise moves to setting sun.
Clouds dissolve and re-evolve as clouds.
Every hour ticks toward the start
of one more hour
and another after that.

Even progress stumbles, disappears,
reinvents itself and reappears.

The price of life is death.

Eighteen Songs

Solitude's My Home

Above the pounding of the rain,
beyond the rolling of the sea
A thousand people know my name,
And one or two may yet know me.
There in the middle of the night
I'll find a friendly face,
And I'll be taken back again
to some new loving place
And, no, not left alone,
Although solitude's my home.

I try to beg the hand of help
Sometimes when silence gets too rough.
All I can offer is myself,
That never seems to be enough.
And yet there are some men who kill
for less than someone's hand,
At some things I can only guess
and never hope to understand.
No, I'm not alone,
although solitude's my home.

Faces there are I've never seen,
faces there are I'll never see.
But what a waste it would have been
To have been anyone but me.
Still if I sound a little proud,
My head will often bend
on seeing someone in a crowd
I'll never hope to comprehend.
No, I'm not alone,
Although solitude's my home.

I turn my face toward the wind,
and shuffle down the darkened street.
With winter coming on again,
there's no telling who I'll meet.
Perhaps a love will open up
and hold me for awhile.
Who knows what waits within the night.
Beneath the surface of a smile,
No, no, I'm not alone,
Although solitude's my home.

Written in Los Angeles, 1972

Many Summers Ago

Girls in summer dresses
sighing summer sighs
girls with warm and willing smiles
why do you pass me by?
You wouldn't think so
to see me now
but I was loved once.

You wouldn't think so
to see me now
but someone really cared.
Many summers ago that was
many summers ago
when the trees were budding
and the sun was high
nobody passed me by.

You wouldn't think so
to see me now
but I was wise once.
You wouldn't think so
to see me now
I thought I knew it all.

Many summers ago that was
many summers ago
when the trees were budding
and my hopes were high
nobody passed me by.
Imagine me, the bachelor of hearts
the last one to leave the ball,
imagine me with the world in my arms
then summer turned to fall.

You wouldn't think so
to see me now
but I was young once.
You wouldn't think so
to see me now
but I was a little boy.

How many summers ago that was
many summers ago
when the sun reached out
to the top of the sky
and I didn't know how to cry,
and nobody, nobody
ever passed me by.

Written and composed in New York City, 1960

About the Time

About the time,
about the time you've decided
you know all that there is
along comes some teacher
with a new kind of quiz
a new kind of wanting
and you've nothing to give
but your time

About the time,
about the time you've decided
surprises are few
you awaken to find
that the new day is new
you reach out to touch it
and it runs off in the night
chasing after some new face
with a far fresher mind
and more of time's time.
About the time, about the time.

About the time
about the time that you find love,
pay love some mind at all
you learn that each spring
has a summer and fall
and love, like time's pendulum,
swings to and fro
and you go home alone.

About the time,
about the time that you bend love,
bring love to its knees
the poor wounded heart
looks up one day and sees
love running like lightning
through your lifetime
on its way out and you find yourself
wondering what the shouting's about
It's about time, about the time.

About the time,
about the time that you learn life
you've burned life at both ends
and the old need for living
like the need for love ends
and you find yourself staring
at the same wall again
marking time.

If there were time,
if there were time I would tell you
why time is a thief
stealing moments then minutes
then hours and weeks
leaving nothing at all
for the heart and the mind
but the slow endless pounding
of years into time, lifetimes.
By that time you've run out of time.

Written in Paris and Rio de Janeiro, 1974

I've Been to Town

I've been to town,
I've walked the highways
and the harbors too,
I've done some things
I never thought I'd ever do.
Now as I stand here
looking down at you,
you ask me why it is I frown,
I guess it's 'cause
I've been to town.

I've been to town,
beyond the boulevards
and down the beach,
I've learned some things
that only time can teach:
For instance, love is more
than just a little speech,
it's got to find a common ground;
I know because I've been to town.

Don't tell me any more lies,
I can't waste any more years.
I've seen my image in your eyes
dissolve in disappointed tears.

I've been to town.
You ask me do I know
the Milky Way? I do, and furthermore
I'd like to say, it isn't milky white,
it's dingy gray, especially when
your worlds break down;
I know because I've been to town.

Written and composed in Los Angeles, 1962

Empty Is

Empty is a string of dirty days
held together by some rain
and the cold wind drumming
at the trees again.

Empty is the color of the fields
along about September
when the days go marching
in a line toward November.

Empty is the hour before sleep
kills you every night
then pushes you to safety
away from every kind of light.
Empty is me. Empty is me.

Written and composed in Rome, 1968

When the Bars Close

The hours after midnight
are the hardest ones to kill
up a dark street, down a dark street
                    all is still.
It's lonely after midnight
no matter where you are
when the evening starts
and the evening ends
around the corner
at the neighborhood bar.

One more drink, one, that's all.
Hear the waiter yell *last call.*
Tell me please, I'd like to know
where do people go when the bars close?

I'm new in town but I've been around.
L.A., Frisco and some other towns,
same old story everywhere you go.
Where do people go when the bars close?

You can't see stars
through this ceiling
but gee it's warm in here
even though the plaster's peeling
the pace has a kind of cheer.

I talk too much, so I've been told.
Pardon me for being bold,
but maybe, no I don't suppose,
you'd care to go with me when the bars close.

I live up three flights
number five in the rear.
The ice box isn't working
so you'll have to drink warm beer,
if you care to go with me when the bars close.

Written and composed in New York City, 1960

April People

April people try to smile
even when they're sad
because they know
behind the rainbow
things can't be that bad.

April people all are lonely
that's the general rule
and more than once a lonely heart
has made an April fool.

Born in April, sad of heart,
you're a lonesome child,
but you could make the sun shine
with even half a smile.

April people live for love
nothing else will do.
So come along and take my hand,
I was born in April, too.

Written and composed in New York City, 1979

Me and the Cat

We've seen so many winters come
and watched so many old years go
and held so many hands at dawn
we never really got to know.
Lying down someplace shady and flat,
me in my shirttails, him with his whiskers
                            me and the cat.

We've done so many foolish things
and yet the days have served us well.
We've given all our smiles away
for they were much too good to sell.
Livin' the good life without gettin' fat,
me in my shirttails, him with his whiskers
                            me and the cat.

Looking back, few friends had we
but I've got him and he's got me.

And when the golden minute comes
when we no longer wake to smell
the river where the wild swans sailed
the orchard where the blossoms fell,
we'll smile a little thinkin' of that.
Me with my whiskers, him with his whiskers
                            me and the cat.

Written and composed in Antibes, 1966

Sommerset

Every day was Sunday
and every month was May
and every girl who came along
was sure to come your way.
How many years ago was that
ten, fifteen or more
when we lived at Sommerset
in that time before?

That time before we grew so big
before we grew so tall.
Before our eyes were wide enough
to see beyond the wall.
How many years ago was that?
It seems so long ago
when we lived at Sommerset
and watched the summer go.

There's a cold wind coming
I can tell.
Blowing back the memories
of times we loved so well.

When we lived at Sommerset
a life or so away
every day was Sunday
and every month was May.
How many years ago was that
ten, fifteen, or more
when we lived at Sommerset
in that time before?

Written and composed in San Francisco, 1967

148

Thank You

All the taxi horns
have sounded their retreat.
The wind is down to nothing
but a whisper in the street.
And now as you lie sleeping I'll take
a moment just to tell you
all the things I never say
when you're awake.

Thank you for the raspberries this morning
and thank you for the orange marmalade.
And last night let me say
when you might have gone away
thank you very much because you stayed.

Thank you for the sun you brought this morning
even though the sky was full of clouds.
And thank you for the way
you held me yesterday
and steered me through the noisy Paris crowds.

I can't look ahead to the future
and I'm too old to run home to the past.
So now while you sleep on beside me
I'll do what I can to make this moment last.

Thank you for another special morning
and thank you for an even better day.
And thank you in advance
if there's even half a chance you'll stay,
one more morning. One more day.

Written and composed in Amsterdam, 1965

Blessings of the Day

For every day that I may live
I'll keep a smile upon my face
because you put it there for me.
And should misfortune come along
I'll shrug and send it on its way
and count the blessings of the day, my love.

A blessing on the rain that falls
a blessing on the wind that blows.
I'll not forget to bless the lovers everywhere
and those who stumble, those who fall
grant a blessing to them all.
Let them see the face of God and love.

Bless the animals and birds
bless the blue and velvet sky
not with words but with the comfort of your eye.
And for the children everywhere
let them know how much we care,
let them see the face of God and love.

For every day that I may live
I'll keep a smile upon my face
because you put it there for me.
And should misfortune come along
I'll shrug and send it on its way
and count the blessings of the day, my love.

Written in Edinburgh, 1972

My Brother Edward

My brother Edward's always there
and that's the way it has to be.
I love him and he loves me
My brother Edward's always there.

Half of nothing isn't much
and yet he's half of all I am.
God must have made a master plan
My brother Edward's always there.

When we were growing into men
I never needed mate or friend.
The good and bad that people share
I shared with Edward, he was there.

Now as the years begin to slow
and each is counted out and done,
if I can count on anyone
My brother Edward's always there.

My brother Edward's always there,
his shoulder's strong, his eyes are sure.
I couldn't get from here to there
unless I knew Edward was there.

Written in Sydney, 1982

154

Love, Let Me Not Hunger

The bumblebee goes
from the rose
to the marigold,
then goes back to the rose.
The caterpillar climbs
each ribbon of vine
even the caterpillar knows,
the day's so warm
you wouldn't dare touch it
if it lay down by your side.
So come to me, come to me,
my arms are open wide.

Love, let me not hunger—
I've been alone so long.
How can a little taste
of wine be wrong?
We'll not get any younger.
Come listen to my song
and if you've had a hunger
perhaps you'll sing along.

The day's so warm
you can feel the sun.
What does it matter
what's done in the day
after the day is done?

Love, let me not hunger.
Come and take my hand,
and if you've ever hungered
I know you'll understand.

*Written and composed in Malibu
and Los Angeles, 1964*

156

So Many Others

Comfort me with apples
torture me with tears
make up for the lonely days
and all the lonesome years.
Place your little fingers
here within my hand
there've been so many others
who didn't understand.

Bring me pretty marbles
the best that you can find,
sing to me of rivers
it helps to ease my mind.
Talk me pretty love words
and I will do the same,
there've been so many others
who didn't ask my name.

They'd look at me and wonder
what is he thinking of
when all I ever wanted
was lullabies and love.

Tell me that I'm handsome
and lots of other lies,
come along and love me
with little summer sighs.
And even if you leave me
pretend your love is true,
there've been so many others
there might as well be you.

Written and composed in Sausalito, 1963

If You Go Away

If you go away
on this summer day then you might as well
take the sun away; all the birds that flew
in the summer sky, when our love was new
and our hearts were high; when the day
was young and the night was long, and the
moon stood still for the nightbird's song.
If you go away, if you go away,

But if you stay,
I'll make you a day, like no day has been
or will be again; we'll sail the sun,
we'll ride on the rain, we'll talk to the
trees and worship the wind. Then if you go,
I'll understand, leave me just enough love
to fill up my hand.
If you go way, if you go away,

If you go away,
as I know you will, you must tell the world
to stop turning till you return again,
if you ever do, for what good is love
without loving you; can I tell you now,
as you turn to go, I'll be dying slowly
till the next hello.
If you go away, if you go away,

But if you stay,
I'll make you a night, like no night has been,
or will be again; I'll sail on your smile,
I'll ride on your touch, I'll talk to your eyes,
that I love so much. But if you go,
go, I won't cry, though the good is gone
from the word "goodbye."
If you go away, if you go away,

If you go away,
as I know you must, there'll be nothing left
in the world to trust; just an empty room
full of empty space, like the empty look
I see on your face, I'd have been
the shadow of your dog if I thought it might
have kept me by your side.
If you go away, if you go away.

Written in San Francisco and Brussels, 1964

Gone with the Cowboys

One day, with any luck
I'll be off again
gone with the cowboys
on the high roads and then
bulldoggin' sunshine
the way I should have been
all these years that I mistook
for livin' settin' in.

I only hope too much time ain't gone by.
I may not make Montana
but I'll give it a hell of a try.

Soon as the snow clears
I'll be off again
gone with the cowboys
playin' poker with wind
not thinkin' no more
'bout how it might have been
I'll be in there livin'
with the cowboys again.

Sure as the sun sets
and the world rides on the wind
I'll be ridin' somewhere
with the cowboys again.

Gone with the cowboys again.

Written and composed in Cheyenne, 1970

The Last of the Wine

I lie here dying
in a hundred small ways
from voices crying
my name down nameless hallways
and the clock keeps ticking
eating up the time
and I'm down to the last of the wine.

My stomach growling at the movement
    my hand makes
in reaching out toward
the disappearing handshapes.
Dreams come true, everyone's but mine
and I'm down to the last of the wine.

And I crawl on my belly through the night
and I dream of dying in the sunlight.

As unseen shadows
in the morning start to harden
I rise up singing
to the angel in my garden.
Some dark and different
angel of another kind
and I'm down to the last of the wine.

And the angel never taught me to pray
and I die with the dying of the day.

Written and composed in Hydra, 1968

Times Gone By

Remember how we spent the nighttime
counting out the stars.
Too late for the beach,
too early for the bars.
All of us together
would raise our glasses high
and drink a toast to times gone by.

The times, oh we had some times
when the world was the color of neon signs.
Each of us and all of us
killed our dreams with rye
and tried to crowd a lifetime
into times gone by.

Remember how the Sunday morning bells
were always ringing
and out along the waterfront
we'd hear the big men singing.
In some long-forgotten time,
some August or July.
Even then we'd talk about
the times gone by.

The times, oh we had some times
when love cost only nickels and dimes.
Always when our secret needs
were hard to satisfy
we'd talk of going back again
to times gone by.

Remember how we talked and laughed
and cried into the dawning
and the terrible taste
of kisses in the morning.
Crowded rooms and lonesome tunes
and very little sky.
Even then the better times
were times gone by.

The times, you know we had some times
with gentle women and vintage wines.
But that was when we didn't know
our youth was passing by.
Now all we have to think about
are times gone by.

Written and composed in Sausalito, 1963

Index of First Lines

169

About the Author

Rod McKuen was born in Oakland, California, in 1933 or 1938 (he has two birth certificates of record). At eleven, he left home to work and help support his family with odd jobs that took him throughout the western United States as rodman on a surveying unit, cowhand, lumberjack, ditchdigger, railroad worker, and finally rodeo cowboy. His first attention as a poet came in the early fifties, when he read with Kerouac and Ginsberg at San Francisco's Jazz Cellar. After serving two years as an infantryman in Korea, he returned as a singer of folksongs at San Francisco's Purple Onion. Before becoming a best-selling author in the 1960s, McKuen had been a contract player at Universal and a vocalist with Lionel Hampton's band and had amassed a considerable following as a recording artist and nightclub performer. His books, numbering more than forty titles including *Stanyan Street & Other Sorrows, Listen to the Warm, Beyond the Boardwalk, Celebrations of the Heart, Lonesome Cities,* and *Caught in the Quiet,* have been translated into some thirty languages and make him the best-selling, most widely read poet of his time. His film music has twice been nominated for Academy Awards *(The Prime of*

Miss Jean Brodie and *A Boy Named Charlie Brown).*
His classical works—symphonies, concertos,
suites, and song cycles—are performed by
leading orchestras and artists throughout the
world. *The City: A Suite for Narrator & Orchestra*
commissioned by the Louisville Orchestra, was
nominated for the Pulitzer Prize in Music in
1974.
He has written songs for nearly every important
performer in the music business, producing
standards that include "If You Go Away,"
"Seasons in the Sun" (both written with French
composer Jacques Brel), "Love's Been Good to
Me," "Jean," "I Think of You," "The World I
Used to Know," "Rock Gently," and "I'll Catch
the Sun." Those compositions, among others,
have earned the writer-composer-performer more
than forty gold and platinum records worldwide.
He is considered one of the few major
performers than can guarantee "sold out"
concerts in whatever country they choose to
appear.
   Despite his many ongoing careers, writing
occupies most of his time. Rod McKuen poetry is
currently taught in schools, colleges, universities,
and seminaries around the world. He is recipient
of both the Carl Sandburg and Walt Whitman
Awards for outstanding achievement in poetry.
With nearly forty million books of poetry in

print, the author has no intention of resting on his laurels. He still writes "every day of my life" on the road, in the rambling Spanish California house he shares with his animals, or in his part-time "digs" in Australia. He is currently finishing a book about his experiences in the Soviet Union, where he composed the mammoth score for the twenty-hour long television documentary, *The Unknown War.*
The Moscow Philharmonic has just recorded his Symphony No. 3 in C minor.